MORE THAN Moons & Chinese COOKIES

MaryPat

ISBN (Print): 978-1-09837-659-8
ISBN (eBook): 978-1-09837-660-4

TABLE OF CONTENTS

DEDICATION

To our biggest cheerleaders:

Shana
Joseph
John
George
Mary
Sally

We succeed because we immerse ourselves
in the many-layered mantle of your love and support.

Thank you.

PART 1:
Peace or Pieces?

written remnants

unwrap pieces of days
some silk
ultra-suedes
madras bled
written 'round melon rinds
river buoys
undoubtedly
more than moons and Chinese cookies
irregular regular stuff
10,000+ days
collectively wrapped remnants
blown together
random pieces
pieces of pieces.

Ladybug and the Leaf

The pin oak leaf landed
Shiny side up
Gently held steady
In the slight movement
Of the protected eddy.

Ladybug landed softly
The leaf barely moved,
Or so it seemed.

Yet just that motion
Put leaf in motion
Oh so slowly.

Ladybug fluttered
Her transparent wings
Happy to take a moment
To sunbathe quietly, resting
Before resuming her journey.

The flutter jostled the leaf
Ever so slightly, into the flow.

The leaf now in motion
Still stable, but slowly rotating
With Ladybug perched in its center
Undisturbed by the slow motion.

Leaf drawn closer to the main current,
To a much faster, stronger flow.
Passenger seemingly unaware.

Then, caught in the current,
The leaf rotates much faster.
Another splash in the current
Lands water drops on the leaf.

Ladybug flattens her legs
To keep the delicate balance
And tries to shake off the droplets
That weigh her down.

Undeterred, both leaf and current
Pick up their pace.

Leaf swirls faster and faster,
An unstable footing for Ladybug launch.
Then crashes to a halt
Against an immoveable boulder.

Ladybug launches upward
Gains solid footing on dry boulder flattop
Shakes her soaked wings
Holds them out to dry
Settles against the sun-warmed surface.

Leaf now torn into pieces
By flotsam thrown against boulder
Wedged in place by current's rhythmic pressure
Leaf shreds disappear under on-rushing water.

Ladybug, now dry and warm,
Gracefully lifts off to
Resume her life's journey, too.

Performing a Vibrant Life

She has a presence; a stately aura
A polish and patina both inherent and learned
A smile that bathes exquisite features
In warmth, light, and sparkle.
Her presence vibrant with passion.

But it is her mode of speaking
That captures your attention.
Her smooth, precise delivery and tone;
Each word carefully chosen before spoken.
Her voice strong, clear, and clarion.

She loves the language of the academy.
Embraces new words from across disciplines.
Adapts her theoretical expertise to new research
    perspectives.
Revels in discussions of potential studies and explorations.
Her mind continually inquisitive.

She honors her cultural roots and diversity
Through her styles, clothing colors, and accessories;
Through stories of history and heritage.
Her descriptions vibrant with life and breath.

She tells of her struggles, as a woman of color.
The academy had not welcomed her warmly.
But SHE knew she belonged, regardless;
That the theatre of academia would bring evidence
Of her stellar performance.
Her story one of determination and grit.

She cultivated her extraordinary niche
In the vast arena of human communication
Focusing on how people perform their lives;
On African and African American stories
Of cultural history and transitions.
Her worldview: the African diaspora.

She restructured her focus to include issues of health
From Black barbershops to beauty salons
With stylists and clients and an eye to family impact
She brings health research and expertise
To African American and other communities of color.

Known throughout the City by her networks and
    connections
This woman of presence and polish and substance
Brings a message of resiliency, and strength, and
    health focus
To an audience unused to emphasis on its wellness and
    well-being.
Her message grounded in strength and resiliency:
Believe and persevere.

Tests of Tensile Strength

Inherently funny, 'tho she seemed unaware
Edgy sly humor; rapier wit
Ready for laughter although often quiet, until
Embracing both art and science with equal aplomb
Her father's pride and joy.
All this we saw while, in her mirror
She viewed the world as a serious backdrop.

She looked petite and fragile
Against the massive bulk
Of the sorrel Belgian stallion
Sleek white mane and tail distinct
Highlighted with rosebuds and braids
His ears swiveling forward
To catch her gently-voiced directions.

Braving ice, snow, and long lab hours
Hunched over assignments and books
Watching microscopic changes
Sifting, sorting, measuring, separating
To unravel the mysteries of each helix
To find answers to her questions
And new insights for those upcoming.

Now challenged by the new world of life;
Wife + mother + scholar + teacher
In new surroundings; under new conditions;
Within new environments, both professional and social
Looking forward, anticipating, expectant
Building a full life of family and friends

Looking with amazement at a new generation
Of professional women—so different since the 60s!
Neither accepting nor bound by 50s expectations
Not easily integrated into existing systems
Assertive, outspoken, challenging, but hampered
Often disregarded, dismissed, dismayed, appalled
At existing rigidity, and not quiet about it.

She seemed so fragile; nearly translucent
Blocked from light from any source
A mother's worst fate; a near fatal blow
A family bereft; a daughter now gone
A son deprived of a younger sister
Subsumed by guilt out of context
Heart-broken upheaval and onslaught
Followed by seemingly bottomless pit of empty.

Then time. And more time. And even more time.
Marched on through the emotional destruction
Toward a plateau of life reordered
Toward a time of fewer self-recriminations
Toward a restart of purpose in daily life
While raw edges lessened from blood red to scabbed
    over pink
Remaining vulnerable to unanticipated reminders
That tore the wounds open again.

A welcomed change in position and goals
These with college-wide implications, strong outward focus
Department representations, program successes,
National standings and student recruitment at stake
With emphasis on advising this new generation
Teaching and coaching goal-setting and career path selection
Advising on professional audience expectations
Mentoring, encouraging, reviewing, supporting
Guiding toward the future with gently-voiced directions.

A nudge back into the wider world
A broader web of professional interactions
The need to encourage more academic prowess,
Pulsing new life into old settings.
Reaching out to national colleagues
Discovering new regard for her person
Uplifted by others' regard for her professional standing
Lifted to leadership; centering the health provider web
Expanding prospects for students
Strengthening determination to continue on.

Moving toward individuality; a professional identity.
What a change!
New persona acknowledged by both town and gown
Building support for a third generation of health
    professionals
Advising them on critical advancement strategies
For academia; for next steps; for purposeful life; for success.

Her son moves on; college, jobs, marriage;
Doctor in his own right; following the mother's model,
Practitioner, teacher, advisor, health professional.
His mother still his affective anchor
But, he's now also more part of her strength
Side-by-side with his father,
Anchoring her in focus and purpose.

A strong family unit once torn asunder re-glued
Quietly tackling each day as it comes
Ensuring abundance of love, loyalty, and laughter
Even now guided by her gently-voiced suggestions.

The Gown

At some distance in diffused light,
In voluminous folds and pleats
Fanning out from tight-fitted bodice
Skirting of subdued green velvet spreads out in all
    directions.
Topped by rich chocolate polished stones invisibly
    connected
Shiny and reflective, depending on light placement.
White, frothy shawl, translucent here and there,
Air movement changing its folds and rolls
Surrounds golden-hued spire of gleaming clasp.

Upon closer inspection under bathed light of day
Indicators of visible wear emerge
Blotches of besmirched velvet materialize from the shadows
Obscuring rents in hollows of scalloped fabric layers.
Broken edges of stones adhere to ornate brown bustier
Some left shiny; others bludgeoned into ragged surfaces
Unable to reflect light or display hidden crystals
Tell stories of forces beyond mortal control.

Under withering heat of unseen challenges cottony mantle
    dissolves.
Pendant now shines of mauve, lavender, and rose
Mirroring stages of changing light beyond.
Velvet elegance now diluted; reflective gems now muted;
    shabby edges now softened
Snap to silhouette against diminished illumination,
Blackened shroud disguising form and boundaries,
Waiting in finite darkness for renewed radiance.

the 1 & only official kindergarten sepia print

mother had
to send that awful
picture, a rescued 5" x 7"
ripped across the hairline
yellowed tape
    off gray
    off black
    off brown
    off white
1 & only official
kindergarten sepia print
circa, class of '49.

me
  I see it in glorious memory color
    A little girl 49 lbs.
    A big left ear braids limp
    Bows barely
    Freckles fading
    Lips chapped, cracked
    Teeth...3 missing
    And those eyes
    2 big blacks with lashes curling
    And the 6X dress, voile of
    A palest pink and eyelet white. . .

but
   would you believe in all
those days of 'education'
that day
and only that day
     I threw up
     threw up
     threw up my lunch
and half an hour later
     "click". . .

The photographer caught it
     mother bought it
     I ripped it
     she taped it
     saved it
and
22 years later
had the nerve
to send me
     the off gray,
     off black
     off brown,
     off white
official
throw up at school day
picture.

Dahlia

I first noticed her
One summer day.
A singleton amidst
Darker "royal" colors.
Her rich coral tint
In contrast.

She held her bloom high.
Tho' she was quite small
And much shorter than
Sunflowers towering over
Other garden growth.

Her presence
Magnified by
Her solitude.
Expanding bloom
In perfect balance
On her sturdy green stem
With solid emerald leaves
As her bouffant skirt.

Concentric layers of perfect
Coral-hued petals
Cupping orange-yellow
Stamen cushions
Of soft pollen
Landing pad for honey bees.

Fall temperatures arrive
And still she stands
Her post alone.
Now contrasted with
The darker remnants
Of summer garden gone.

I marveled at her
Tenacity in the face
Of oncoming winter
Foretold by night time
Cold and daytime rain.

The weather broke.
The sun shone bright.
And there she stood
A beacon among
Ravaged garden
Of summer.

The frost came on, of course.
But daily sun warmed us both.
And lingering dews left
Her leaves sun-sprinkled
With droplets of condensation
Like diamonds on emerald velvet.

Colder nights brought frost
Near freeze to our world.
Her leaves in sunshine sparkled
In delicate droplets
From melting warmth.
Her leaves in shade
Covered in a shimmering coat
Of crystal sequins
Spinning prisms of rainbows
Upon dense foggy air.
Each curled petal
Rimmed in crystal lace.
Her most magnificent
Costume of all
As she danced in the
Cold winds of winter
Before being covered
In the whiteness
Of glorious endsong.

Delicate Deception

The creator perches
At the very hub
Of the intricately constructed design
Delicate symmetry geometrically balanced.

Twenty-six gossamer columns
Extend and expand
Into trapezoidal wonders
Long edges anchored
To nearby structures
Ladder-like steps top to bottom
Stretching between column edges.

Glistening magically
In bright sunshine
Or in subdued light
Inviting passing travelers
To alight in beauty
To take a moment of rest
On their journeys.

Unknown to enticed voyagers
The danger of glistening gossamer
The strength of intricate design
The purpose of anchored columns
The worth of graduated stair steps
The intent of pathways from the hub.

Then came the windy buffet
The columns strong withstand
The following rains drench
Drops strain the fibers before falling
The design sustains
The creator waits in suspension
Securely balanced.

The sun returns
Insect world activity resumes
The creator alerts
To the renewed energy of travelers
As a swarm of wings
Flutters to a stop
Among the gossamer filaments
And the creator lifts up
Aligning each of eight legs
Into positions of speed.

The goal of trapezoidal wonder
Of intricately designed structure
Of strongly anchored columns
Of cross-threaded steps
Of glistening gossamer strands
Now realized.

Cacophony of Color

The palette of mountainside Spring
From chartreuse to olive to emerald
Reflections bouncing from glistening pin oak
To subdued matte olive desert trees
Interrupted by shouts of color
Red-orange flames spiking above
Strands of miniature circular shapes
Only green and bushy after rain.
Palest yellow of mountain dogwood
Whispers beside sunburst yellow of palo verde
Towering over deep golden wildflowers.
Not to be outdone, undertones of darker greens,
Mesquite, juniper, and cedar, create cover for
A lower timbre of resonate deeper green
Leaning downward to embrace
A crescendo of flowering cactus petals, en masse,
Topped by waxy yellow expansive blooms
Snapped almost immediately from their juicy buds
Outbursts of birds seeking the essential nutrition
Of each petal's fruity sweetness.

This empire of cacophony overseen by stately saguaro

Spiny arms aglow with clustered bloom-filled crowns

This brilliant white plumage displayed only

While sunlight is brightest each day

Overshadows the pastel shades of arms and spines

These royal statues of the desert mountainside

Lending shade to the vibrant purples, pinks, and oranges

Displayed across the pitch of the desert slopes,

Framed by multiple tones of flora.

eye of 4 o'clock light

Pause
on the bank of the barbwire divide
and
look through the eye of 4 o'clock light.

The house
night and day
shingled in gray with
tight storm windows that
pitch electric yellow shadows on day old drifts

Creamed drifts reach out for smothered barns
and touch
in a 24-hour Christmas of frost-faded red and
tin-roofed green.

An unseen horse whinnies.
four Angus smoke in uneven formation
two brown sows chaw peanut brittle ice
looking east Squaw Creek eats along snow-grown hills
circles a stop in my mind.

This collage alive and living in Iowa.

honeyline

On the wet edge of sand
feet imprints dissolve
as the river water
strokes the shore.

Nearby a shell lies open
a spackled cone within
an iridescent ear—an echo of soundings.

Cans aluminum lites
submerged sculptures once
bled river towns' beer brews
perfect cylinders—now trashed.

Algae cattails bulrush burr reeds
all Nature's ribbons waving wavering
weaving almost a wedding bouquet
    green brown
    green brown green

All along the wet edge of sand
this sunlit honeyline
holds the shore's debris.

PART 2:

Curiosities

Tree Treasures

The sound of the wind
Through the pine forest
Grows closer
Sounding much like
A wave moving toward shore.

The straight trunks of tall pines
Begin their slow, circular pattern
Of counter clockwise motion
As the wave of breeze arrives.

Movement uncovers tree-bound treasures
The squirrels' home, way up high
Anchored by a web of limbs and trunk
Displays careful weaving of twigs and soft grasses.

While raucous jays sound their chatter, too,
From their smaller home, further down
Carefully built between branches
It sways easily, yet firmly, in the on-coming wind,
Seeming to understand the preciousness of its content.

The wave moves past, to farther places
It's distinctive sound fading in the distance
The tree's treasures disguised, once again.
Gentler forest sounds emerge.

nameless kite

kite
squeeze the ground
in the bend of your toes
suck-suck a belly
full of air
rush so high
hang in a breath of April
drop
let go
taste daisies white
sip with the bees
tip—your seersucker tail
hug—your balsa stem
make a wish
soar.

Mysteries in the Mist

The outside light dimmed
Low hanging clouds obscured the sunlight
Moving across the pine forest
Laying a gray layer upon
Vibrant glistening greens
Towering totems of age-old growth.

Thunder rumbled and boomed
First afar and then nearby
Windows shake with reverberation
Incoming air sharpens and freshens
Lightning flashes grow close then quickly fade
Leaving behind the fragrance of ozone.

Squirrels scamper up tall trunks
To carefully constructed nests high above
The incessant chatter of jays and crows
The buzz of locusts, bees, and wasps
Now unheard.
All movement ceases
Silence descends. Waiting.

At first, the oncoming wind
Can be heard rolling through the forest
From the distance it moves,
Setting the treetops of the forest in motion
Roaring above all living things
Leaving underbrush quivering
As the sound arrives and passes
Propelled to unknown destinations.

The curtain of rain follows on its heels
Driven through the tall pines
Sharp needles slicing each drop
Into gently flowing mist
Floating downward to cover
All shapes across the forest floor
Weaving a mysterious backdrop
From ground to lowest branches.

Once clearly defined shapes
Now filtered into indistinct shapes
Now seen as mysterious creatures and objects
Redefined by each intermittent gust of wind
Renewed by continuing onslaught
Brought by pounding rain curtain
Adding another layer of needle-sliced mist.
Tarp covered woodpile seems to move
By Giant's strides as waves of material
Powered by the rise and fall of wind gusts
Entangled Manzanita bushes sway
As large cumbersome beasts
Barely maintaining balance against Nature's force.
Underbrush sits unobtrusively in the mist
Not tall enough to catch the wind's attention
But moving just enough under the weight of the rain
To add mystery to the mist-filled world.

The fixed straight ears of the prickly pear
Stand ready to fight with its spears and loaded balls.
The occasional tumbleweed appears from nowhere
Catching, stalling, rolling, vanishing into unseen spaces
The bull elk antlers, majestic in scope and spread
Add dimension and movement among low hanging branches
Barren tree limbs, all akimbo and black outline,
Bring skeletons to this scene of shadows and murk.
Outdoor lights become mystical glowbugs
Haloed in mist; seeming to move without fetter
Through branches and bushes already in motion
Disappearing then reappearing in various locations
Guiding only the movements of undetected adventurers
In attendance during such a clime.

From the silent mist following the downpour
A horse emerges, unnoticed until this moment
No sound of hooves on rain-soaked ground
Rider bent forward; hat pulled down to deter rain.
Tack now dark brown from extended exposure
Saddle blanket covered with small leaves and twigs
Horse moving resolutely forward, reins slack to saddle
    horn wrap.
Unmindful of human misery, the horse conveys a purpose
As it moves steadfastly back into the mist
And disappears, once again.

In a reversal of fortune, the mist lifts to reveal
A sparkling green carpet covering the forest world.
The statuesque pines showing off their
Glistening green coats of needles, freshly laundered.
The low hanging gray clouds replaced
By patches of blue sky and radiant sunshine
Mysterious shapes once again well defined
Nature's bright light unhampered by gloomy gray clouds
Reveals the newly-washed world aglow with freshness.
A contented sigh emitted by all who observe.

eye of the moon

While March rapped
we lay on the mat
in the wool of the tent
and the scrub
and the sand
and the ledge in the rock
echoes the mountain cub's sigh.

Beneath us
lit by the eye of the moon
a shadow appears
then movement
silently a beeman waxes
in motionless motion.

We view his path
through the bee swollen lot
combed in the neck of the womb.

He emerges again and again
through the honey-swelled acre
grafted in bliss to the hide of the hill

Silently we watch
the beeman waxes
in motionless motion.

Bless you.

Ideas in Flight

Ideas arrive by various means
As may have been observed
Different avenues of flight
Catch the attention of the curious.

Some ideas crash into being
Some float as on a cloud
Some meander, elevated by air
Some swim down the lazy river
Others get swept up in the torrent.

The fly ball careens over the back field wall
    and the flight engineer catches the notion in flight
The final note of a rabbi's chant carries new meaning
    to the composer's new sonata
The meteor streaking through the darkness
    prompts the astronomer's bright idea
The raven silently winging over the tall forest trees
    brings the sound engineer insights
The bright red maple leaf floating through Fall air
    offers the slash of color to spark the artist's eye
Fighter planes streak through the sky, sound left far behind,
    to inspire both eye and mind of those who catch the sight

Fragrances of Spring blooms saturate the air before
        penetrating thoughts of the perfume maker
Honey bees skipping from bloom to bloom scattering flowers'
        pollen spores buzz into the vision of the crop duster
A helium balloon escapes from the small hand, and lifts
        small wondrous eyes into imagined heights
The final note of a song in the silent theatre resonates
        in the future of a violin student
The final call to prayer from the minaret echoes
        in percussionist cadences old and new
The sailfish flies through the air from somewhere under
        to somewhere under, spawning the amphibian invention.

The contrail of the commercial jet
Overflowing with human ideas
Streaks across the limitless sky
To wherever it is that ideas go, in flight,
In a somewhat desperate search for
Receptive, inquisitive minds.

Beckonings

Don't like the weather right now?
Just give it a minute.
A popular saying in the desert Southwest
Where mountains, valleys, heat, cold, deserts, and plateaus
Mix in a palette to nurture all tastes.

Don't like Winter cold and snow?
Just drive straight south for 2 hours or so.
Don't like oppressive heat, even with no humidity?
Just drive straight north for 2 hours to reach tall pines beauty.

Love warmth, color, blooms, and floral fragrances around?
Just find your way to the Valley of the Sun; a place many
    people have found.
Want immersion in borderlands history and lore?
A trip to the southern territory will quench that thirst.

The Old West abounds in the southern desert towns
And in the mountains that surround lies history
Of the ancients, the explorers, the adventure seekers.

Is Native American culture more to your liking?
Then look all around you, from Mexico border to the
    North Rim
For landmarks, artifacts, and amazing displays
Of artisans' work in leather, gemstones, and clay
Of oils, and charcoals, and natural dyes; media grounded in
    Nature's eyes.

If the flow of great rivers makes your heart thump
Then the mighty Colorado to the west beckons you.
If sand dunes perfect for ATVs and boards are your targets
    for fun,
Then the SW corner gives you chances to get sand in your
    shoes.

Want rolling hills, green valleys, and fine wine?
The SE quad will rock your travels through green hills,
    dales, and times.
To ranches and vineyards of local acclaim,
And B&Bs, hotels, and places the Old West still claims.

If the majesty of canyons gives you great pause
The north and northeast wonders are stunning in scope
Integral to the history of all, these landmark "living"
    wonders
Lift spirits, give breath, generate awe
Reminding of past, both of Earth and of Man.

Expand your perspectives of immensity and might
Of Nature's power around us, even if out of sight.
To an horizon of ranges across desert flats and cacti
To peaks dusted with snow that don't look all that high,
To mysteries hidden off trails of old,
To fantastic stories, told and retold.

Follow those beckonings to new places and thoughts.
Embrace the unknown and unknowing as adventure,
Allow mental wanderings to prompt interest anew.
To each temptation to find out, to search, to discover,
Just let go and do!

I hear asparagus count my toes

I'm me. . .
only 3
my plot's 3' x 5'
the dirt's dirt
and black
and wet
and sticks to my hands
and grabs my hoe.

look all over----
see the oak roots
border the cloth's poles
as the brick porch
holds the 2 o'clock sun.
now look over here,
see 'em pair off.

pair off the hollyhocks and asparagus
and the honeysuckle and rhubarb
wait. . .
the birth of buds
follow single file
in a parade roll of smells

I stop
with my head
locked to my knees
to see
the hollyhocks hang from
the bridge of my nose
feel rhubarb tickle my thighs
taste honeysuckle juice
stuck to my tongue while I hear, yes,
I hear asparagus count my toes.

Remember. . .
    I'm me
    only 3
    but my garden is 3' x 5'.

Curiosities in the Woodpile

A flash too quick to verify
Was something there
Or did my eyes deceive?
I halted my trek to warmth and comfort
Wondering if I might have an adventure
In store.

Slight movement betrayed
A presence
A pair of green eyes
Blinked at me
From between pieces
Of seasoned firewood.

In a forest, green eyes are everywhere
So, no surprise, a second pair
Appears suddenly in next chink down.
A family or siblings or playmates?

An exploration is required.
My movement met with
Scurrying sounds
Behind the rain-soaked logs
To my surprise
Came big black eyes
Shining through the upper
Woodpile spaces
These eyes bright and sharp
And not so curious and wide.

I stopped my progress
Looking closely
At my observer
Assessing viability
Of closer inspection.

What of any size
Could be sheltered there?
Should I disturb any shelter
Exposing it to the cold and wet?
What life needs such disruption
To please my curiosity?

As if in answer
To my internal queries
I heard scrabbling noises as
Two small bodies
Scrambled up the backside
Pointed ears and bright eyes
Peering over the top log.

Their adventurous move
Drew a low rumble
From the pile
And all movement ceased,
Including mine.

Then more eyes
Looked out from chinks.
Some small, like those above
Others larger, like might a growl emit.

A family, then, found refuge here
Outside my forest refuge.
My curiosity quelled
My questions fully answered
I returned to my original mission
Of making my way inside to
The warmth and comfort
Of my shelter in the forest.

I waved to the small ones atop.
I nodded to the large ones inside.
I backtracked to my nearby refuge
While watching this new neighbor
With smiles in my head and heart;
Taking comfort in sharing life spaces.

Desert Still Life

Spectacular in its barrenness
Sandy soil, spans of brown and white
Grass bleached white under day-long intensity
Of unbuffered sun and wind.

Dust devils, small and towering
Whirling into view out of nowhere
Escalating to wondrous heights
Before encountering outflow
From rows of tall desert cyprus
And stands of cooler cottonwoods.

Unbroken views to horizon
Miles upon miles, acres upon acres
Of sameness, but only on the surface
Or to the glancing eye.
Closer observation reveals otherwise.

For high above the hawk slows and circles;
The crow already on alert.
These carrion mark the presence
Of other life. . . and death
In seeming lifeless territory.

Then comes the dusk and larger life
Of elk and deer and oryx
Emerging from outer shadows and slopes
While coyotes yip-yip
From brushy dens.

The desert "still life" day-long painting,
The monotony of sun and wind
Gives way to sound and scuffle
Bringing life to those lands
That seemed so lifeless hours before.

Air War

Against azure sky with slowly floating scattered clouds
Swooping motion among the pines
Almost too quick to follow
With the naked eye

Breast to breast, inches apart
Flaps at 70 per second
Both summoned by the sight of fuel
Territory to be declared and challenged

They face off vertically in mid-air
Assessing, announcing, appraising
Flash of green; ring of white
Standoff momentary
Whirring almost soundlessly

Before one makes his move
Into loops and drops
First dodging left
Then circling right
With challenger inches behind

Beckoned by red highlighted by sun
A target known to all
The dog fight follows naturally
A hierarchy only the flyers know

All around the target
The space becomes a battleground
Of stamina and superiority
For territory and authority
Over access to the target
The source of life for all

Each flyer loops down, strafing the target
In hopes of finding time to stop and refuel
Surprised there by strong resistance
A second flyer swoops in from the left
Driving the first back into the sky

A third arrives with no fanfare
No flash of green, no ring of white, no breast of orange
But just as fast and just as determined
Rewarded by a clear path to the targeted fuel
Ignored by the fight-in-flight warriors

Meanwhile the warriors fly their loops, dives, and dodges
Each target pass a sign of power
Neither gives up space or speed of pursuit
While the third maintains the species

At last a break; one is deterred
The victor alights upon a branch right above the target
Secure in guarding his hard-won space
Until his next challenger arrives

This microcosm of living life
Performed as tragedy,
Or comedy, or ignored as unimportant
Depending on the view

Yet mirroring the behaviors
Of the world of animal species
Warriors, challengers, dog fights
Proclaimed supposed victories
Repeated, repeated, and repeated

While those maintaining the species
Go about that unheralded
Repeated, repeated, and repeated.

PART 3:

Rhythms

Waves

Waves wash over; alerting senses
Rolling toward; rolling over; rolling away.

Waves of golden grain; shining, reflecting
Gently bowing before the temperate breeze of summer.

Waves carrying sharp sounds of Fall
Rustling dried corn stalks and sharp-edged leaves colliding.

Waves upending shiny aspen leaves
Flat, matte surfaces quiver; rain coming.

Waves greeting shores, having arrived from afar
Passing over geology, archeology, biology; creating
    musicology.

Waves lapping to shore, licking at the sand
Bringing treasures to land; change back to seas.

Waves crashing against cliffs, scrubbing surfaces
Causing chaotic surges, back washes, breakage.

Waves up-ticking in speed, rolling in peaks and troughs
Generating rhythmic highs and lows of pounding surf.

Waves of wind-driven rain lashing blades of grass and
    massive limbs
Pausing momentarily to allow life to drink and breathe.

Waves of wind-driven snow obscure earth's blemishes
Drifting in glamorous layers of glistening sequined white.

Waves of gauzy clouds across the full moon
Being nudged by puffs of winds aloft, between earth
    and orb.

Waves of echoes in caves, tunnels, canyon walls
Confirming actions of Nature or Man, or both.

Waves of human emotion know no barriers or differences
    between
Releasing gales of laughter, screams of grief, shouts of joy,
    howls of devastation.

Waves of human hello greetings and goodbye leavings
Universal body language taught, learned, understood.

Waves of lifeblood pulsating through trunk and limbs
Ebbing and flowing, again. . . again. . . again. . . .

one Christmas present

The night before the calendar Christmas
You, tree, stood alone
a green glow
lights strung in a hapless maze
blue flashes
bells circling ready to hang
silver-sided tinsel, still boxed

You tree, poised to glow
through the window
alone in your half dress
smell of Christmas past
dandelion wine and homemade stilts.

I see somewhere out there
snowpile-packed winter scenes
of Christmas last
Mr. Cooper Claus high again
on the breath of his "Ho Ho Ho"

I see Story Street Variety Store gifts all
for the saved coins in my wet green mitten
figure skates over frozen toes
holding raggedy dolly painted happy
midnight Mass

A green glow blue flashes
pieces of past memories flock your branches
smelling of bayberry days
of Christmases long past

I see me.
I see you, tree
wait together
share tomorrow
one more Christmas past.

The Cycle

Thunder clapped
Then came rain
Then the breeze
And then again.

Every droplet split
By tiniest branches
Creates forest mist
Making shapes hard to define

Thunder claps
Then comes the rain
Furrows made
Cross lands reclaimed

Creeks again begin to trickle
Forest floor greenery begins to grow
Greener banks alive with creatures
Water of life comes with the flow

Thunder clapped
Then came the rain
And then the breeze
And then again.

Spring Foals

The broodmare pasture was ready
Awaiting new mother mares and foals
Carpeted in soft new clover
Racks of newly mown fragrant hay
Newly piped and filled water troughs arranged
Buckets of grain mixed with sweet molasses
Hanging from fence posts
Spaced to allow room for each mare.

First residents from the foaling barn
Arrived in early Spring
From rich brown bay to cream-colored palomino
With like-colored foals with wobbly legs in tow.
Then came a blue roan, a paint, and a red sorrel
Accompanied by foals just as colorfully diverse.

Soon the pasture sported an array of colors
Some matched, mother and foal, mostly not
All side-by-side at hayrack, water trough, and feed bucket.
Territorial issues clearly defined by each mare.

Afternoon brings a lull.
Foals find warm soft spots for napping
Often splayed out flat; knobby legs extended
Mares standing guard; sometimes adjusting to give shade.

Afternoon naps over, colts play.
Like small children of all animals
They run, chase, spook, and cavort
Mares feed while watching
Sending signals when needed: nickers, snorts, soft nips.

Shadows fall over the pasture.
Dew cools the clover blanket
The mares gather their foals
And move to the gate,
Ready to return to the barn's warmth and comfort
Their safe haven during the still-chilly Spring nights;
Protection from Nature's weather and predators.

Monsoon Music

Dancing limbs, first east then west
Air recast from blue to brown
An orchestra of nature's instruments
Produce a monsoon symphony.

Elegant Dancers

Attire reminiscent of more formal times
Bouffant sleeves amid others
Shaped as pillow puffs
Or trimmed in lacy, spider-like fringe.

Rustling juniper bush crinolines
Festooned with white berry pearls
Complimented by shiny oak leaf corsages
Aflutter at each movement
The mystique of ages in 100-year dancers
The newness of only decades in younger growth.

The graceful movement of multiple dancers
Circling counter clockwise through space
Elegant arms clothed in deep green apparel
Transparent or opaque or mystically both
Depending on perspective and view.

Stately presence in form of
Ballroom dancers
Arms out; Backs straight!
Ready to move to rhythms
Yet to sound.

The air is still; no music yet
Only sounds of rustling anticipation
Reach ears of ready listeners
Awaiting cues to step and swing.

Then, from the distance
Come first notes
Alerting dancers to prepare
To gain their stance
On floor of softest greenery.

Closer and closer
The rhythm sounds
Brought to dancers
On wings of wind.

Arriving at full volume
Propel the dancers
Arms in motion
Crinolines in full sway
Bodies in coordinated moves
In counter clockwise flow.

The music fades
The dancers return
To centuries-old poses
Under cerulean skies.

A Pod's Life

Spring rains push life through trunks, branches, and leaves
Prompting new growth and life
While summer breezes ensure sun and light to all
Sunlight streams on opening buds
Seed pods begin to form
Anticipating role of rebirth
Fall winds strip leaves
Branches bare but for pods
Bobbing, finishing, browning, readying
A surprising gust dislodging
Flinging far and wide
Propelled by launch from catapulted branch
To crash in some unknown locale
Exploding to expel the seeds
That, with coming Spring rains,
Will be coaxed into new life and growth.

Quiet Love

The small form emerges
Black double wide doors as backdrop
Part of the immense glistening white barn
Rain soaked slate roof reflecting spears of sunlight
On lightning rod spikes at roof crown

Moving up the hill from barnyard to driveway
Balancing 2-gallon stainless pails
One for each hand; a strong arm needed
Filled with frothy fresh milk
Followed by 2 barn cats and a kitten
Moving carefully up the slope

The crunch of steps on limestone
Signaling a more level surface of driveway
More sure footing and closer to the 2-story matching
    white house
Inset decorative side porches topped by shining slate roof

Progress along the stone driveway
Each step carefully taken
Confidence of long practice evident
Cats and kitten close behind her heels
Hoping for slosh or spill

Without shifting attention
Movement catches her eye
A smile emerges, eyes twinkle with love
Smooth motion forward never stops

"Are you hiding?"
Answered by a child's cackle-giggle
The waggling trumpet vine
Dances as the child launches from behind
Giggle-cackle paired with hop-skipping
All motion and joy
"Come along then."

Skip-hopping child, scooping up kitten
Golden ringlets bouncing with each happy step
Grasps an apron corner with left-over hand
And joins the parade
To the expansive rear porch

Milk dishes filled with fresh warm milk
Cats gathered around the edges
Sounds of happy lapping
Kitten carefully placed beside mother
Woman and child disappearing inside
Screen door softly slapping frame
Before latching.

Singular Purpose

Delicate swan neck with distinctively shaped pod
At the tip of the slender fragile branch
Dipping and rising in spates of gentle puffs of breeze
Breathing in gulps of life-sustaining air,
Up and down, swaying rhythmically
'Til pod drops to soil below
To begin new life.

The Power of Six

The thunder of two dozen hooves
Shod in heavy iron
The rumble of steel-wheeled wagon
Echoing off tunnel walls

The roar came first
As audience gasped
At the power of six
In full gallop

Harness slapping in extra motion
Across shining chestnut bodies
Tanbark spewed in all directions
Driver's lines in perfect sync

The collective gasp exhaled
The applause and whistling began
A perfect 8 made from end to end
Before time for them to stand at attention

The driver's smile from ear to ear
As he doffed his jaunty fedora
To claps, shouts, and whistles
While snorts and head shakes from decorated heads
Acknowledged the crowd's acclaim

Upon command all motion stopped
The crowd, now silent, absorbed eye-catching details
Of rosebuds and ribbons on white manes and tails
Of strings of white rings and rows of brass rivets
To color-matched wagon of old-fashioned design

The judge carefully examined each hitch and each horse
Giving directions to each driver for moves to be made
Pull forward, then back up
Stand, all feet aligned; heads straight ahead
Complete attention in pose and set

Then came the hitch
That had captured all hearts
Its horses, their power, the audience awe
Its beauty and style—perfection, in art.

The crowd let its roar
Tell the judge how it stood
The big smile reappeared
The hat tipped, once again

The challenge now met and bested that day
The hitch remained at attention
Awaiting command
The driver spoke softly to keep them at steady
His love and pride heard in his words

At last it was their turn
To leave the arena
The crowd stood again
Cheering loudly for more

The driver and horses
Obliged their admirers
Around the coliseum they moved in smooth rhythm
Again, the perfect 8 brought audience cheers

Then straight to the tunnel
They aimed as a unit
And the thunder subsided
The arena quiet once more.

Black on Gray

Black forms sailed into opaque grays
Disappearing momentarily
In the churning clouds of mist
Boiling up from the pounding surf
Crashing into ship-size boulders
Sending spray in all directions
Coating all shapes nearby
In small, wet, salty-flavored currents
Dashing back into the sea.

More Black forms take definable shape
Settling on lonely singular limbs
Stripped of leaf and green
Jutting out over roiling clouds of mist
Angular, ethereal, and starkly dark
Against gray profiles and black silhouettes
Of surrounding surfaces and features.

Ragged cliff outcroppings
Dangerously diminished and muted
Sharp promontories along the shore,
Appearing less ominous
When blurred and smudged
Through moving veils of gray haze
But somehow known
To forms in flight.

Above the mist-shadowed realm
Closer to highest cliff protrusion
Several forms took discernible shape
Settled together on branch and limb.
Facing outward toward brisk breezes
Singing their song of life and breath;
A chorus calling out to the ocean.

Rhythms of Silent Snow

The deep indentation in the snow
Rapidly refilling edges already blurred
Newly deposited flakes piling up.

Gray woolly skies blanketed
All paths, trails, tracks
Settled in as if no amount
Of airflow would push them aside.

No sign of sun, albeit day
Muted light of Winter sun
All sound muffled or silenced
By a blanket of glaring white.

Life moves without notice
Small prints, trailing tracks, cloven hooves
All covered quickly, unnoticed,
By fine powder of Nature's paint.

A flash of brilliant blue sears gray toward white
Bursts of raucous chatter split the air
All movement halts; prior silence accentuated
No answer but a flutter of scarlet through branches.

The silence breathes again, without sound,
Inhale; exhale; all living things.
Life's flow resumes across fields and through trees;
Unseen rhythms now magnified by absence of interruption.

PART 4:
Tangled

once—
an innocent

do I remember
that not so little girl
with the lavender scent
and all that hair
always
hiding that pale brown eye
the one
rejecting the contact lens?

was it, really,
just so far ago
and long away
or just too too many
yesterdays?

the sun hung in her sky
her moon
and at least 100 stars
controlled her nights.

she was the red fuzzy
bear coat, top of the line, of course,
that led the cheers
for Ol' Notre Dame
Iowa... ... Wisconsin
and caught, god forbid,
the tight end from Illinois
—but that comes a bit later.

back in bock beer bar
—sout' side Chicago.
she danced
and danced
and danced.

in the classroom
she studied
literature and language
wondered at philosophy and physics
skimmed humanism
and discovered
the psychology of performance.

then the little girl, almost 21
with the innocent dare
took up
with the Illinois
All American Boy
all 6'4"
sweater green eyes
With a smile polished thrice daily

Thus began
the grand flight
or was it the great race
some, unkindly,
called it the proverbial
chase?

and
like all great epics
she mused
"I think I'm in love!"

She opened her heart
and he spread
his Illinois All American
charm—he liked her
    as well as his saved baseball card heroes
    and his tales of flying pucks

the flight-fight
race-chase
continued and continued
love/lust comingled
with study times for
LSAT and GRE.

After an overstimulated time-out
he summarized their session
with five terminating words:
"Us?"
"Engaged?"
"Married?"
"NO WAY!!"

He moved on.

The girl with the lavender scent
wallowed along alone
too too many tearful nights
no star gazing consoled her.

that innocent girl
with all that hair
watched
the sun in her now vacant sky
counted
her own stars
and met her academic challenges,
even her GRE score.

she gradually found herself
she realized she had choices. . . choices. . . choices. . .
she discovered a new life path
of her own
she saw that love. . . is love. . . is love
First Love being just a first.

that was
yesterday
yesterday long gone
was it really
so long ago,
or so far away,
or just
too too many yesterdays?

always
bougainvillea's bloom

just you and me
an armful of letters
phrases of praises
promises of passion
how
many ways
can I say
"I love you!"
2 lives printed
in blue ink pages

his monologues
airmail or special delivery
when the rain crashes
snow freezes

and always bougainvillea's bloom
that moment
today… those weeks… this month
phone charges
an' charges

what do ya' do
solutions… alternatives
trade a city of lights
for a desert of stars
wait… remember…
decision time. . .
where wolves howl
if the full moon joins us?
yep—just you and me.

Classic Roadster—vintage 1958

I know
the grunt and bang of a diesel start-up
the classy limo sigh
the cough and burp of a 4-speed coupe
but you, little egg,
vintage roadster
shell of wax and soul-red leather
you come to me
with genuine screech of brakes
and gas-fed rush
Stop.
Bring me my man of
too-full days
occupied mind
attaché bulging
Cellphone holster
Little egg
little egg
Stop here.

February AKA 3rd month

Adam & Eve
coiled in question
folded
molded
on spackled illusions

blue cotton daisies
circled
in yellow
bled
from the flat
of the land.

Saturday roses

rose
do you remember
who plucked you
snapped your stem
pressed you to his grip
did you feel him hold you
did you see his eyes light
when I reach out
did you feel us touch
did you share the moment
did you hear us
talk about you
the dialogue
"How do you know they're for you?"
"Silly, I'm stealing them from you."
a laugh… a shared time
love time.

enclosed is a piece of rose

enclosed is a piece of rose
a year ago it was part of a whole
and many roses gathered to bunch
He offered them to HER—one month of love
love came together on the side of the mountain
and that day and the next
and the season continued
and that love grew
    on island "A" trains
        camel towers
        duck lakes
    and deep heat rubs
The HE and SHE became parts of a whole
    today is one year and one month
    SHE offers to HIM—a piece of rose.

Memo to a VIP Lover

Sir:
Our time…
not to be confused with
your time, my time
children's time
work time
Board time
Y-time, running time
or even football time
cannot be separated
segregated or spaced
on a calendar
of special events
sacred holidays or
secular holidays.
Our time is prime time;
prime time is now.

wedded souls

we
neither end nor begin
but
evolve
a pretzel round projection
weaving…wavering
a woven golden band

immeasurable pleasureables
related
in unrelated intangibles

fused
to circular laterals
profusions
emulsions
wet silhouettes
blown
to silent charades.

love and care

"Do you mind?"
We fold in an oversized chair
an undersized bed
I march
all over your body with a possessive eye
making verbal notes.

"Darling, your baby curls need cutting."
"You have a bite under your arm."
"Did all those scars come from being a little boy?"
"I'm going to taste your birthmark."

Monologues fade
You look at me
I swim in your eyes
Nonverbal communication takes over
Silent sounds
    "Do you hear me?"

in so many words

you
don't have
to say you love me
but
it would help
if you could show it
show and tell
or
tell by showing it.

enough

enough, enough multi direction
is it me?
is it you?
both of us
move
in multi direction
too many questions
you say, "petty"
me that talks
you that stares
me that cries
you that glares

too many questions
too much talk
following you
or
leaving me
here
we go 'round in multi directions
no more
no more
I stop.

all those somedays

we used to laugh
at certain songs
and always
talked of someday
someday. . . someday. . .
someday when I got 30
    when I cut my hair
    when I become a writer
    when I sell an oil
    when I stop the pill
someday when you get famous
    when you redo the roadster
    when you get the serious camera
    when your youngest goes to college
    when you divorce
someday would be the best time
    to wed our souls
    and last forever. . .

that someday kind of love
  never came together
    I got 30
    kept my hair long
    stopped the pill
    earned a byline
    you reached even higher
    raced the roadster
    published your photos

a whole lot of somedays
  ran together
each of us
  making choices
  creating
  celebrating
  our separate somedays
then
one random day in a regular elevator
  sans clever dialogue
  I said, "Hello, Mr. C."
  and you replied, "How nice to see you, Mrs. T."

and you a bit thinner
glasses thicker
60
aging
and me
41
humming that certain song
me, not a fading rose
but elevator music always
brings out those lyrics
--for me--
just remembering
all those special shared somedays
went somewhere
with that long gone
someday kind of love.

when you gotta' say—"good bye"

do I
spill the emotion
well the commotion
cracks crunch
crumbs crumble
--"good bye,
 heart breaker"

The Gift of Connection

She was, at first
Another friendly smile
Welcoming us to our favorite
Breakfast place
Where we are "regulars".

Like others there
She came to recognize us
Ask after us
Take special care
Of us.

Until, one day,
A gauze bandage appeared
Between her shoulder and neck
New worry lines
Around her eyes
Prompted us to inquire.

Cancer treatment, she stated
To begin the next week.
Misted eyes all around.
She would continue to work
She would lose her hair.... Maybe?

But she would, she declared,
Beat this thing!
Agreed! We responded.
Time to "kick butt and take names".
"You've got that right!"
She smiled, determined.

The weeks went by
We checked, every one.
She held her ground
Sometimes tired; always brave!
We cheered her on
Sincere good wishes
And hugs (no pandemic yet).

Then came the virus
And the doors were closed.
We hunkered down
Like all we knew
And hoped for the best
'Til we could get back.
. . . And then we could.

Outside we sat
The safest choice
She wasn't back
The concern in our voices
Met with assurances
And then, through the door
She came
To our delight (and relief).

Her tests were clear
Her energy palpable
Her vivaciousness back
Renewed with a fresh beginning.
Her smile visible,
Even behind the mask.

Now on to her next adventures
She goes
Healthy, happy, and ready
It seems
To follow the new pathway
To her next dreams.

We wish her the best!
First, get lots of rest!
Then start down the list
Of what you don't want to miss
Knowing we thank you
For sharing your life
With us.

blue bird

She glided in gracefully
Lighting on the railing
Fluffed her pastel grey-burnt orange feathers
Fanned her blue-grey tail
Took a balancing step
Before settling
A patch of color on green.

She cocked head
At the human nearby
Then looked left, then right
Smoothed her breast feathers
With her beak
Enjoying sun and breeze.

He swooped in to land beside her
All bright blue and orange
On full display
She ignored his interruption
He puffed his brilliant orange chest
Fanned his bright blue tail feathers
Spread his wings, pushed next to her
Ignoring the human nearby.

She shook herself
As if rebalancing
From the force of his presence
The push of his wing
And settled, once again
Unruffled, unperturbed, uninterested.

He was dissatisfied
His "routine" ignored
He tried again
Poofed out chest
Fanning impressive tail
Pushing closer.

She turned her head toward him
A quick beak thrust to his head
A sharp chirp in his direction
Before she lifted soundlessly
And vanished into the forest.

He sat there, still
All blue and orange
On full display
With none left to impress
Except the human
Who still watched.

3 girls turn 39

3 girls turn 39
3 girls look 39
—give or take
3 girls talk of '62
and
a few choice years between
highlight 20 years
with a 4-hour lunch

safe to share
caesarian births
braces for teeth
3 houses
a boat
7 daughters... a son.

careers
stopped
pending
proceeding off course.

weight
gained
lost... rearranged

blush brushed on
   Over smile lines
   Crow's veins
   Aged acne
   A frown
but, always smiles
no caps.

3 girls couldn't
quite mention
the baby born before;
the anorexic middle child;
the Black Irish.

those husbands
all 4
the one that still played
the one that stayed
the one that inevitably
moved on
the one long gone.

lovers un-Catholic—
move on.
safe family ties
sisters well married
the League
brothers in law:
Money, Money & Money PC

the fathers
that died
almost canonized
ah, the mothers
nearly cloned.

3 girls coming of age
together again

couldn't be
20 years
oh, well

smile
the cheerleader grin

pass the brie
and yes,
a bit
more liqueur.

The Strong Hand

He had a plan for each of them,
His children numbering three.
He'd lost one before any of these
Expanded his world
That pain making him doubly vigilant.

He had a plan for each of them.
It centered on success in life and work
Based on strength of character
And courage to take on risks

He had a plan for each of them.
He knew the strengths of each by three
He knew what needed built and nurtured
Where to push; where to practice;
Where to wait and see.

He had a plan for each of them.
The context of the family farm
Gave opportunities galore for him
To direct, to teach, to set (and reset) the bar.

He had a plan for each of them
With love it's central core.
He cheered, cajoled, corrected, and challenged
To foster learning, mastery, and more
In-depth thinking with a critical eye

He taught them love of nature
And how to care for animals and others, first.
He taught them love of languages
The rhythms and the songs of words.
He taught them that learning was important
Every day no matter age, or space, or place.

He loved to laugh at jokes good and bad.
His stories kept them entertained
Whether hard at work in fields and mows
Or bagging wheat or chopping corn.
He kept them busy, building strength
Inside and out, character and form.

The kitchen table was the place
Where he tied it all together.
He confirmed the links between work and play
How one made better the other
How both were essential to successful life
How love of family was "the topper."

He had a plan for each of them.
Imagine his surprise to find
That on this road so carefully designed
For individual cherished child
Each had built a plan as well.

Their plans included love of life,
Of solid proof they knew themselves
Of work and play and strength to fight
Of love and learning and roads to success
To places he never would have guessed.

He had a plan for each of them.
He wasn't sure theirs were the best.
He fussed and fumed and interfered
He worried his guidance had not been enough
To keep them on the paths
To the dreams he had for each of them.

He had a plan for each of them.
Each chose a different plan and path,
But each emerged as he had dreamed
Strong, determined, caring, driven,
Laughing hard, working hard, loving life
And to his amazement and everlasting awe
Teaching others with a similar firm hand.

scents

Wearing sweet rosebud
Waiting for the 1st dance
With a waist-cincher bra
A crinoline slip
And garters with stars
AND YOU?

Wearing mimosa scent
Waiting for the 103rd St. bus
Warm in wet trenchcoat
A term paper in progress
And calculus—overdue
AND YOU?

Wearing a full-blooming gardenia
Waiting for a "hat trick"
With 2 layers of woolies
Midst a howling crowd
His eyes on the puck
AND YOU?

Wearing an enchanted fragrance
To compliment my bouquet
Waiting for the wedding vows
Almost a life time—what can I say?
NOT YOU!

Wearing tangerines and lemon
Waiting for the hail to stop
With the tent leaking
2 schnauzers burrowing
And him asleep
AND YOU?

Wearing the forbidden perfume
Waiting for the 'red eye'
Surprise, surprise
He's with yet another 'stew'
AND YOU?

Wearing none of the above
Waiting in divorce court
2 irreconcilable years
Good-bye heart breaker
AND YOU?

Wearing shower fresh
Watching through the weeping willows
Balancing on a ladder
Stringing Chinese lanterns
Suddenly a steady hand
Then 1st kiss. . . Great Gods!
Fireworks & stars
and
the ultimate question:
IS THAT YOU??

5 Decades

5 decades passed
But each still knew
The other's voice
And speech patterns, and
Pauses.

5 decades past
They had common ground.
Beliefs shared
Pastimes shared
Love of the written word
In all forms
Shared.

5 decades passed
Marriages (plural for both)
Children (plural for both)
Singular now, again,
Emotionally and in heart
Though by different causes
Under different circumstances
And unnamed after-effects.

5 decades past
There would have been
No hesitation
No anxiety
No heightened anticipation
At the thought of
An in-person encounter.

5 decades past
They would have known well
The important places to go
The newest things to see
The finest food in town
The best places to gather
To sit and talk, at ease
The most comfortable church
For Sunday Mass.

5 decades passed
They acknowledged
A need to meet again.
Time to reconnect
While making space
For safe advance or retreat
Without knowing which
Each might choose.

5 decades passed
Somewhat hesitantly
In the first words
Of greeting
In the first smiles
Exchanged
In the first sentences
Uttered.

5 decades passed
They thought they'd feel different
Now
That life's journeys
Had reworked them
Tissue and bone.
That challenges
And adventures
Irretrievably altered
The connection.
Until they held
Each other's hands
Again
Now.

5 decades passed
They knew they looked different
Now.
Except when they looked
Into each other's eyes
Again
Now.

This Bed & Me

The bed had a history
Before me, I know
Because it was there
Before me, I know.

It was there when I became me
My first moments on earth
The first time cradled
Outside, not inside.
My birthing bed.

By all guesses of ours, chosen by a woman
Of elegant and sensitive tastes.
Chosen for its luxuriant warmth of color,
Its gentle curves and skillfully crafted features
Of welcoming comfort.

It may have held, delicately,
A young woman of dreams
Unknown to later wish for faraway places.
Before being assertive was OK.

Or, held the one remembered as "a sweetheart"
The favorite sister and aunt of grandfather before
Family-bound and happily so
Watching over brother's family
With loving thoughts and shielding care.

Delicately formed, burnished rich brown
Maple, maybe; or, oak, perhaps
Smoothly contoured headboard
Reminiscent of gentle waves
Some scrolled peaks, then curving away.

Spindled columns at the head
Gave support for waves and swells
Four corners held by spindled posts
Carefully formed and polished to sheen by use
Footboard echoing headboard curves
Sideboards, too; simplicity in design,
Striking, in effect.

This "three-quarter" bed, as it was known
(People were smaller then, before me.
'Tho not in character or purpose!)
Reminded all of history, of family long gone.
Of restless ones, of steadfast ones
All come before.

But now the bed birthed "family"
One by one, at least for three
And then re-assigned to host the girls
After crib and on to college.

From frost on counterpane in winter
To April showers pounding on windows
Through thunderstorms and microbursts
The bed steadfastly awaited our return

It welcomed us exhausted, from barn and field
And harbored us when illness struck.
It cloaked us from tumult and fear.
The staple of our emotional diet.

It's squeaky springs comforting, in their way.
Wooden slats repositioning the weight
With sounds of gentle friction
Against the solid framework
A calming rustle to soothe frayed psyches.

One off to college only lightened its load
The other bound by history stayed
It seemed we were connected still
By stories shared and yet not told.

Setting one to wonder if. . .
Listening quietly would reveal
Whispered stories of the mystery
Of past souls embraced.

And so it remains,
Seven decades and some later,
And more years to come, together,
This bed and me.

Shared Silhouettes

Backlit by the diffused beams
Of yellowed streetlight
A black silhouette of tree skeleton
Clear through the foggy dark.

A system serving as conveyance
Of life and sustenance
Waving slightly from intermittent
Puffs of heavy humid air
Propelled by night breeze.

Trunk as primary arterial conduit
Thick, substantial brace as
Branches emanating from trunk
Extend into dense translucent fog
As if reaching for an unseen destination.

Glistening droplets travel along the limbs
Clinging to the rough bark
Before sliding once again
Toward the end of feathery fingers
Of spidery twig ends
Bouncing slightly in night air
Before dropping to earth beneath
To nourish and sustain
The Mother Tree.

Backlit by the light box
Attached to the office wall
The most recent x-ray
Displays the silhouette
Of a circulatory skeleton
Clearly seen against the miasma
Of living tissue underneath.

Mid-screen, a large artery
Displays as predominant image.
A thick, substantial conduit
Serving a greater system
Of branches leading from this
Main line far into the hazy background
Holding indistinct shapes of organs
And unseen body tissues yet known
To end at definable destinations.

Across the room, a video screen
Displays glistening drops of medical dye
Caught up in a coursing river of blood
Pulsing through visually complex system
Propelled by a rhythmic heart beat
Flowing smoothly through arterial walls
Extending from the main channel at mid-screen
To thinner smaller arteries wrapped
Around and through nearby surfaces before
Flowing into feathery capillaries
Feeding tissues for which these vessels
Serve as lifeblood transport
To sustain the essence of
The Human Body.

PART 5:
Sky Artist

Surrounding Blue Canvas

Across an endless circumference
Of clear unfettered blue
The artist's brush strokes
Bold, solid, striking
Bring bright white waves crashing
Into cliff walls
Sudden upswing of strokes
Denoting end of run.

All this drawing the eye next
To emerging shapes
Backlit by early morning light
Fantastical figures large and small
Translucent bodies, feathery wings
Flowing over elongated trails
Of wispy incandescence.

While in another space
Are dabs of sticky cotton puffs
Thrown against the radiant blue.
Or could those be gusts
Of steamy hot breaths
From those magical species
Seen before?

And on around to next reveal
Stars diminished before light of sun
Silhouettes now clearly defined to the eye
Unveiled, a tattered curtain of cirrus
Dark ominous rains storming through
Powered eastward by prevailing winds
To wash the canvas clear again
Ready for the next display.

an obscure plum light

Through the barbed wire
petrified rows of faded yellow corn
extend pale fingers
to the moon.

Full plum dusk clings low
gradually
spreads a mauve light
stirrings cross the acre.
Ah, a moment for the ruling rooster
to blare.

In response
hollyhocks blow the smell of mist across the field
and
fill the perimeters with sweet reach
of morning dew.

Wind Angel

The translucent cirrus half globes
Forming wings around
The long slender roll of white
Lacy wing surfaces allowing
Spots of see-through blue

Charming cumulus cousins
Jostling for space
In the darkening distance
Beginning the wind-driven race
Toward clear, flat, sunny desert
Ignored by cirrus angel

Wings delicately moving in breeze
In rhythm of gentle undulation
Undisturbed by outflow or updraft
Seemingly unaware of on-coming

Breeze transforming to wind
Distant darkening swoops in
Cumulus now blue-gray boil
Rolling over sand and cactus

Cirrus angel upended, now aware
Arm outstretched trying to halt
Arm pushed back; motion stalled
Leveled by oncoming force

Wings tilt into wind
Angel face-down overrun
Sliding under dark, turbulent force
Gliding swiftly into distance
Wings avoiding perforation
By downward spears of virga
Before desert is swallowed
By summer monsoon.

Roadrunner Escape

The Roadrunner accelerates
Neck outstretched; streamlined
Beak open wide; gasping for air
Cirrus legs spinning like windmill blades
Propelled forward by winds aloft.
Followed close behind by galloping Bear.
Strong downdraft intrudes.
Whoooooosh!
Roadrunner flattened.
Bear lumbers on and over
Completely uninterested.
What bird?

Swimming Sky Creatures

At this moment
The sky artist
Chooses to create
A sea of sea creatures.

Above a bottom border
Of waves of white brushstrokes
Gently pulsed by underwater waves
Appear varieties of sea life.

A smooth-topped cumulus whale
With rounded snout and gaping smile
Two-pronged tail stretched behind
Commands center stage
By size alone.

A small rounded shape
Appears next, 'tho apart,
Away from whale's displacing influence
Then suddenly expands into fierce pufferfish
And dashes forward into the seascape.

The blowfish snout emerges next
It's trumpet-funnel shape a telltale sign
For prey to stay away
Or be funneled up as delicious fare.
'Tho no chance of that in these environs.

Out of whale's view, the sailfish roams
Its movements vigorous, as usual
Causing waves across others' paths
Breaking the surface
Angling smoothly back into the sea
Wet surface featuring fin skeleton
In magnificent profile of grace.

Closer to the bottom a fish of substance
Whiskers stirring up the white brushstroke waves
Moving head and blunt snout
Swinging back and forth
The catfish rummages in unrelenting futility
For airborne sustenance.

Meanwhile the treacherous eel
Slithers in between
It's curvaceous shape easily visible
While its predatory intent
Remains seemingly benign.
No juicy bait within range.

While all are moving in this sea
Carried by lightly swelling air waves
Into their midst; abruptly disrupting
The form of human swimmer intrudes.

Left arm outstretched, nearly to whale
Right arm stretched back in stroke motion
Chopping down on blowfish snout
Kicking feet extended finlike
Whisking catfish whiskers
Shocking surreptitious eel.

Flinging creatures into precipitous flight
Propelling sky waves into tsunami fervor
Throwing shapes into transforming whirls
Churning the sky artist's composition
Into full blown disarray.

The Great Cloud Race

Driven by extraordinarily forceful winds
The great cloud race was on!
Kiting shapes above and beyond.

The first in sight
A submarine
Under full power
Slicing through space
Churning chunks of white
Tossed aside like flotsam.

From above, a skydiver
Arms and legs akimbo
Dropping fast
Then flattened
And driven from view
By windshear unseen.

Now flowing into view
The mighty sleek greyhound
Streamlined lines from nose to tail
Come then gone, almost missed
Because of passing speed.

Not to be outdone, the thoroughbred
Legs pounding forward
Tail straight out behind
Trying to catch up
As afternoon colors
Mark the impending finish.

Then comes the Lion,
Magnificent in his outrage
At the challenge
To his supremacy.
Reared tall on muscular haunches
Jaws wide in bellowing roars
Meant to clear his path.
Backlit by golden sunset
Immense in shape and affect
Warning other racers
To beware of his coming.

Charging against the oncoming
Bank of roiling grey-white
Echoes of the Lion's roar
Bouncing back in thunderous boom
Challenging his kingliness.

Before the setting sun
Changes his light from gold to grey
Before he is swallowed
By the expanding cloudbank
Before all contestants
Are immersed in that tumult
Tumbled, reshaped, dispersed
Spit out the other side
As new visual sensations
For other eyes.

Messenger

Strong featured noble face
Long hair flowing behind
Astride pixilated steed
Of unknown origin

Galloping through cirrus mists
Over stratus canyons
To cumulus mountains
From lands beyond here and now

Reminding of ancestral visions
Of stories told at season times
Life's mysteries explained at fires and lodges
Generations sharing knowledge
Around circles and rocking chairs

Drums adding cadence to movement above
While flutes sing nature's praises
And gourds add emphasis
To voices raised in honor
Of spaces and places

As life moves so do rider and steed
To relatives across all lands and seas
With messages of solid strength and belief
For generations now and seven more.

A Woman of Color

As afternoon blends toward evensong
Arising from the far horizon
Lifted in graceful rotation
By gentle but unexpected updraft
A vertical swirl of color
At once stable, yet constantly transforming
Extending, withdrawing, revolving, circulating.

Swirling figure reveals bright slashes of orange
Amid movements of finely-honed gesticulation
Reminiscent of Fosse choreography
Emphasis in its detail; gripping in effect
Reflecting glitter of silver and pewter bangles
Swinging in ever-changing light

Topped by silhouetted spirals
Seen as a crowd of many
Wrapped in red scarves brightened by shapes and angles
Arms outstretched in celebration
Against a backdrop of sunlit blue they sway
Above a royal blue garment now exposed in new light
A continued whorl in soft rotation
Accented by twinkles from reflective borders
Hoisted by an unseen escalator
To star-struck heights

A final rotation; a transference of light
A sudden twist into billowing embrace
Signaled by outstretched arms bathed in colors
Accented by splashes of amber and gold
From bracelets of cirrus and sunlight
With necklaces in contour and form
Of nimbus reflections
Unleashing scarlet, purple, and fuchsia
Illustrating Nature's compelling artistry
While ushering the vanishing daylight
Toward the lull of eventide.

Perched on golden globe of day's dying light
Still glittering in remaining strong rays
A brilliant flare of emerald shoe
As sunburst merges with blue sea
In a display of primary colors reborn
Before descending slowly into shadows of coming dusk.

The royal blue caftan slowly diminishing in brilliance
Sparkles of jeweled accents adorning its demise
Giving way to the subdued grey-blue of waning sky of day
As stratus formations draw closer
The opaque curtains
Of nightfall.

3 Mississippi Views

October . . .
The hard blue sky
Controlled
No swells of white daring to invade.
October flags... ash... red maple... oak
Wash a tempura slash along the river bluff.

November . . .
The eleventh day of grays
Wrap the barren slough
Grays unwilling to fade
Exhale the river smells.
Only a black night accepts this hollow residue.

December . . .
Same site
Silhouettes
Silent midnights
Almost blue light
Everywhere white
White on white on white.

PART 6:

Reflections

slivers... slices... protrusions

#1 memories
memory slivers slice
my thoughts
protrude
fragments of muted time

past equals present equals
future in sequential disorder

momentary moments
segment
the continuum
the inner me... the outer me
relate in an unrelated labyrinth
slivers... slices... protrusions
fragments in time.

#2 memories
think about us
day... night
our unlit minds
ignite
recreate yellow days
weave on quilted beds
you... me... us
we walk
through a scattered maze
days sewn on a quilt
a formless time
forget
a black patch of yesterdays
broken, caught, knotted threads
slivers... slices... protrusions
in time.

Rooms from Outside Views

Excitement ruled this day of life
The child bounced on toes with joy
From crib to sharing bed with sister
Almost too busy to contemplate sleep
In such a busy grown-up way.

Pillows piled high at edge of bed
To keep young one from falling out
Fresh fragrant sheets from sunshine drying
Warmth from sister sharing
New surroundings to inspect
In morning light.

The Spring breeze lifted
The dotted swiss curtains
'Til they looked like angel's wings
Floating against a backdrop of lush green leaves
And rich-scented lilac blooms
The scents of renewal brushing by.

A newly minted teen stretching luxuriously
On soft flannel sheets under grandma's quilt
Sleepy eyes taking in violets on wallpaper
And a lavender wall framing windows
Before rising to meet the day.

Looking out from college dorm room
Historic buildings on land grant campus
Three strangers sharing space
Drenched in new experiences
Shaping new lives beyond youth

Preparing to find a path
A new life; a new journey
A new beginning; a new identity
Complicated decisions; life changing choices
Forging friendships, relationships, intimacies, and futures
Before the mantle settles on shoulders ready for the world.

Another vista, new surroundings
Singular in this new space of individual choosing and look
Expression of personal likes all around
Pieces with meaning, sentimentality
Arranged for utility, comfort, and warmth
Like early life.

Routine established for workaday world
Choice made reflected in contracts signed
Schedules driven by responsibilities
Real world expectations abound and surround
Preferences exercised only after hours and on weekends.

Compromise makes room for two
A new world of stretch and balance
Another space and place reset
New patterns from combining lives
New visions, structures, surprises
Routines disrupted for newly revealed
Causes, challenges, needs, desires.

A new "family unit" now defined
With three in new first "home"
Again with windows all around
To welcome both friends and earth
To open up to a world of sounds
Brought by breezes laden with fragrances
Delights of world beyond
Experiencing life alongside a new life.

Surrounded by two generations
Now two again, enjoying sights and sounds
Of multi-teen energetic and inquiring voices
Expanding worlds of interest and study
Carving paths through fields unknown in earlier times.

Emerging individuals with profound preferences.
Engaging in life experiences in wholly distinct patterns.
Exercising choices with adolescent fervor and certainty.
Setting goals beyond our knowledge and imagination.

about me

I am
annually
periodically
end of the month
quarterly
sometimes
always
alone.

lake of clowns

Skip a rock
Blow a puddle
Spill a star
Be a clown

Tonight is the night of solo clowns
that mime the air
sing of summer past
summer new and summer last

Two clowns laugh
at their own reflections
in the moon
too high to count the stars
too new to remember

Tonight the night of
silent sand
and
water that breaks in the skip rock time
and
two clowns
connect.

television monologues

Circa 1951

"Captain Continent, do you hear me? Come in clear.
Please don't crash on the Black Planet.
Ranger Ron,
Please be careful."

"Princess of the Four Seasons,
do you braid your hair every day?
Someone said you wore a wig."

"Miss Spirit of the Magic Wand, you really
did see me the day we made papier mache?"

"Commander, the secret sauce added to my milk
makes me burp, but I got the decoder in the mail anyway."

"I can watch you, TV, 'til the 6 o'clock news
then, excuse me, John Cameron Swayze,
I must go set the table."

Wondrous Site

Swirls of white gossamer wafting
Across a layer of azure cream
Lowering then to blend
Into a light layer of whipped whiteness
Atop multiple plum outcroppings
A startling contrast
To an under layer
Of rich brown chips
Mixed into marshmallow texture
In fixed contrast
To cherry red layers below
And then to lower splits
Revealing the richness
Of red velvet
Against steep sides
Of lemon yellow
Sliced through with green sprinkles
And butterscotch-cinnamon clusters
Under piercing bright light
Before dipping deep into
The dark chocolate swirl
Of shadow and shade in Grand scale
Waiting for the next set of eyes
To widen, awestruck,
At the spectacular sight
Of the wondrous site.

A Walk Between Sea and Sky

The weather-worn boards
Uneven, cracked and creased
Much trodden when strong and thick
Now creaked in protest
Of added weight
While soft rhythmic swells
Lapped against aging buttresses
With only the golden rays of sunset
Straight ahead, beyond the dark swath
Of footing.

The sky above a palette of shades of red
From fuchsia to lavender to plum
In bright light, in shadow
In crimson splotches
On pastel pink backdrop.

At the same time, undisturbed below
Smooth mirrored reflections of pier and sky
Painted on deep blue waters
Of calm tranquility and peace.
Serene perfection, doubled.

sweet sweet tomorrow

sweet tomorrow
coming soon
the next featured attraction
waiting. . .

what will it be like
that never never day
have I missed
the anniversary of it?

will it be like the 1st time
can't make
remake
relive... just remember?

the one we bought the red-eye for
San Francisco days
cable car . . . fish boats
nonconformers......... lobster dips
a typical drizzly day
why are we so good
and share
a knowing smile.

ocean blue
ocean green
hold on to that
Palm Sunday
clam chowder air

picture... picture
black & white
see roses red
and Cannery site
smell me
inhale me
drink me
sad...
say, "good-bye".

walk from airport bus
drizzle on my face
tell me
tell me
sweet tomorrow
what will you
be like?

ABOUT THE POETS

MaryPat is a pseudonym for the collaborative efforts of Mary [MaryEllen Zeman-Tinsley] and Pat [Patricia Jo Dustman]. Professional colleagues for nearly two decades, during that relationship the two discovered a shared love of language, storytelling, and narrative verse. Following their formal retirement, the two began to collaborate, creating this volume to share with others. Although the focus of their pieces and their writing styles differ, they discovered that these diverse approaches revealed shared themes and experiences. They hope you agree.

MaryEllen, an Arizona behavioral health expert, specialized in areas of mental health treatment; addiction and prevention; women's health including pregnancy; and, client recovery in many settings. For over three decades, her work focused on leading non-profit organizations in their missions of "serving the underserved" through developing and finding funding for specialized programming, housing, and clinical interventions.

Pat, whose background and experience focused primarily on PreK through Grade 12 public education, spent her nearly three decades teaching and administering public schools in both Ohio and Arizona. Following her years in public education, she joined a prevention research team at Arizona State University where she enjoyed another 2 decades specializing in developing interventions for substance abuse prevention for youth and families.